Che's example opened up for us a broader concept of internationalism

Interview by
Mary-Alice Waters and Luis Madrid

W hen he first met Ernesto Che Guevara in 1957 in the Sierra Maestra mountains of eastern Cuba "Che was already a legend," Harry Villegas told us. "Che was known throughout the Sierra as the Argentine commander who was fighting together with Fidel, admired and respected by the peasants and the guerrillas alike because he was very honest, straightforward, and audacious, very human." Harry Villegas was a seventeen-year-old volunteer joining the small Rebel Army led by Fidel Castro. A few months later that army led a mass popular insurrection that brought down the hated dictatorship of Fulgencio Batista and opened the door to the first socialist revolution in the Americas.

This interview was conducted June 23, 1995, in Havana, Cuba, by Mary-Alice Waters and Luis Madrid. It was first published in the *Militant*, December 18, 1995. Waters is editor of the Marxist magazine *New International,* as well as the books *Pombo: A man of Che's guerrilla, The Bolivian Diary of Ernesto Che Guevara, Episodes of the Cuban Revolutionary War, Cosmetics, Fashions, and the Exploitation of Women,* and other works. Madrid, a staff member of Pathfinder Press, is editor of Ernesto Che Guevara, *El socialismo y el hombre en Cuba* (Socialism and Man in Cuba) and *La última lucha de Lenin* (Lenin's Final Fight).

Today Villegas is a brigadier general in the Revolutionary Armed Forces of Cuba, a veteran of three internationalist missions to Angola between 1975 and 1990, during which he took part in the historic defeat of South Africa's invading forces at the battle of Cuito Cuanavale in 1988. He is the officer in charge of political education for Cuba's Western Army.

Around the world, however, Villegas is more likely to be known as Pombo, the nom de guerre first given to him by Che in 1965 when he was a member of the general staff of the guerrilla forces that fought with Guevara in the Congo. It was the name he continued to use in the mountains of Bolivia in 1966 and 1967, and later in Angola. Following Guevara's capture and murder by CIA-organized Bolivian special forces, Pombo led the six Cuban and Bolivian combatants who broke out of the encirclement and eluded the intense manhunt mounted by the regime for weeks. After almost five incredible months, the three Cubans fought their way to Chile and from there made their way back to Cuba.

Following publication in 1994 by Pathfinder Press of a new English-language edition of *The Bolivian Diary of Ernesto Che Guevara*, we arranged to talk with Villegas about the Bolivian campaign and other struggles he participated in at Guevara's side. Excerpts from Pombo's own daily journal and later accounts by him of the Bolivian campaign are included in that new edition.

In February 1996 the Cuban publishing house Editora Política will bring out the complete Bolivian diary of Pombo, under the title, *Pombo: Un hombre de la guerrilla del Che* (*Pombo: A Man of Che's guerrilla,* published by Pathfinder, June 1997). It includes documents from the Bolivian campaign never before released for publication, as well as Pombo's own account of the months immediately before and after Che's death, based on Villegas's carefully kept diary.

The "honest, straightforward, and audacious" young Argentine commander who Villegas first encountered thirty-eight years ago in the Sierra Maestra mountains was to become a central leader of the Cuban revolution, known and respected in Cuba and internationally as one of the outstanding communists of the twentieth century. For over a decade he would occupy a more and more central place in the struggles through which Cuba's workers and peasants transformed themselves and their society. Mobilizing by the millions they expropriated the interests of U.S. imperialism and Cuba's propertied classes and broke capital's domination. In doing so they began the socialist revolution in the Americas.

Villegas, the tenth and youngest child of a family living in the foothills of the Sierras, was an early recruit to the revolutionary struggle to overthrow the hated military dictatorship of Fulgencio Batista. His father was a carpenter; his mother, who ran a couple of small stores and a bakery in the villages of Yara and Palma, managed to save enough money to allow Harry to attend school.

In December 1956 a small revolutionary force led by Fidel Castro landed on the coast of Oriente province at the eastern end of Cuba. Castro was already a well-known political figure in Cuba. He had been a student leader at the University of Havana, a leader of the opposition Orthodox Party youth beginning in the late 1940s, and one of the party's candidates for the house of representatives prior to Batista's military coup on March 10, 1952. A little more than a year later, Castro burst into national, and international, prominence when he organized an assault on the Moncada army barracks in Santiago de Cuba on July 26, 1953.[1]

Released from prison in response to a growing popular amnesty campaign, Castro and other surviving veterans of the Moncada attack founded the July 26 Movement and from Mexico organized an expedition of eighty-two com-

---

1. Some 160 combatants took part in the simultaneous attacks on the military garrisons in Santiago de Cuba and nearby Bayamo, launching the popular revolutionary struggle to overthrow the Batista dictatorship. The attacks failed, and over fifty revolutionaries were captured, brutally tortured, and murdered; twenty-eight, including Fidel Castro, were tried and sentenced to up to fifteen years in prison.

batants who, with their relatively few weapons, returned to Cuba aboard the yacht *Granma*. They were devastated during their first encounter with government troops a few days after the landing. Those who survived and fought their way out of capture — twenty in all — regrouped and started guerrilla operations in the Sierra Maestra in early 1957.[2]

Word spread rapidly throughout Oriente and the rest of Cuba that the July 26 Movement had launched an armed insurrection against the Batista dictatorship, and that Castro was in the Sierras commanding a rebel army. The news had a big impact on Harry Villegas, then a sixteen-year-old student in Manzanillo. He joined the movement, becoming a member of an underground action and sabotage cell in the city. Soon he was taking part in guerrilla operations in the nearby Cauto river valley.

"We had two skirmishes with the army," Villegas recounted. The second time "we went to the main road and attacked the soldiers, inflicting a few casualties." The army unit counterattacked and surrounded the combatants. When they broke out of the encirclement, they had to head into the mountains to escape, and there they made contact with a squad led by Idelfredo "Chino" Figueredo that was part of a column commanded by Che Guevara.

Guevara had joined the July 26 Movement in Mexico in the summer of 1955. Che, as he was called by his Cuban comrades, had graduated from medical school in Argentina two years earlier. After months of traveling through South America he was drawn to Guatemala, where a struggle was sharpening against the U.S. government's attempts to roll back land reform measures initiated by the government of Jacobo Arbenz. Arbenz was overthrown by U.S. intervention and Che escaped to Mexico. There he met Fidel Castro and he signed on to the *Granma* expedition as the troop doctor. Che was the third confirmed member of the expedition to

2. For more information on the events in Cuba's revolutionary war, see Ernesto Che Guevara, *Episodes of the Cuban Revolutionary War 1956–58,* published by Pathfinder.

be accepted by Fidel; Raúl Castro had been the second. Che's combativity, courage, and leadership capacities rapidly won him the respect of his fellow fighters; he was the first of the combatants to be promoted by Castro to the rank of commander.

While they were with Figueredo's detachment, Villegas said, he met Che for the first time.

"Che arrived on his mule, alone, wearing his cap tilted to one side. He made an extraordinary impression on us. In this first encounter he was very brusque. He asked us what we were doing in the Sierra Maestra, which was very characteristic of him. 'What have you come here for? Why are you here?'

"We answered, 'We have come to fight for the independence of Cuba, to fight the tyranny.'

"'With what?' he asked.

"I showed him a little single-shot .22 caliber hunting rifle. 'You are planning to defeat the tyranny with *that*? No, no, no. You are mistaken. You must go down and disarm some soldiers.'"

Villegas told how they returned to the village to ambush and disarm some soldiers but were betrayed by an informer and failed in their mission. They returned to the Sierra a few days later, however, better armed than before, having persuaded some peasants to give them their pistols and hunting rifles.

"At that point Che accepted us," Villegas continued. "He said we had not completed the mission, but that we had shown our determination to fight.

"Along with another comrade I was assigned to the command post squad and began carrying out the most elementary tasks of a guerrilla unit — going back and forth with messages, carrying backpacks, all those kinds of things — until we had acquired experience. In this way we began to be integrated into the Rebel Army."

Read, study, work, fight

"We became part of Che's personal escort and accompanied him when he was assigned by Fidel to head up the first military school in revolutionary Cuba," Villegas continued. The school for new recruits, established at Minas del Frío in April 1958, was a gigantic undertaking. In addition to receiving training and instruction, the first recruits to attend the school also had the job of constructing the necessary facilities. "We were to build three large barracks, including one for a school and another for a hospital. This was a gigantic effort, because we had to chop down the trees and carry the logs over the hills on our shoulders. And on top of that we had to go to class."

At the time, Villegas said, the school had two instructors. "One was an American named Herman Mark, a big, strong man, very demanding, who was a veteran of the Korean War. The other, named Evelio Laferté, was a young Cuban, a former military school cadet who had been a first lieutenant in Batista's army. He had been won over after being taken prisoner in the second battle of Pino del Agua, if I remember correctly. This was part of the character of our revolution, to win people from the army itself."

Che's authority with those under his command grew with time, Villegas stressed. Guevara's internationalism was an example that struck them all. "Imagine a person who is not from your country coming to offer his life for your country. A man who is capable of that is a man of extraordinary human dimension."

During Cuba's wars of independence against Spanish colonial rule in 1868–78 and 1895–98, many non-Cubans joined the struggle. "We used to view them as foreigners who had come to fight with us," Villegas commented. "Today, after deepening our understanding, we say it is an expression of internationalism. At that time, we saw Che as similar to Máximo Gómez, who was the most prominent of the all the internationalists who assisted us." Gómez, a native of Santo Domingo (in what is today the Dominican Republic) who emigrated to Cuba, served as commander in chief of the independence armies during both independence wars. "In Che we saw someone similar to Gómez, a person who was one of our own, even though he was not born in

Cuba. He had come to help us, to share with us all the vicissitudes and dangers of the struggle."

"Che was a lover of history," Pombo noted, "a tireless reader, a tireless student. The first thing Che did was try to get us to study. Do you understand? It was the very *first* thing! Che liked to surround himself with youth and force us to improve ourselves."

"We combined reading with study: mathematics, Spanish, tactics, guerrilla warfare, novels. The method we used was reading combined with discussion.

"We looked at many aspects of our history, but above all we examined the need for unity in the face of imperialist aggression. We studied the lessons of the revolutionary struggles of 1868 and 1895 against Spanish colonial domination, and the writings of José Martí.[3] We saw how Fidel was able to bring many groups, many revolutionary organizations together in support of a single aim, thus guaranteeing unity of action. In Che's study of Cuban history, he thoroughly studied the question of unity; he analyzed it, and used this history to guide us. At that time we didn't understand the question of unity very well. Today we understand it much more deeply."

This was the process, Pombo explained, through which "we began to become seasoned cadres, to be forged as guerrillas, even though we still had not received our baptism of fire. I had fought as part of a guerrilla unit before joining the Rebel Army, but we still had not been in combat under Che's leadership."

That baptism of fire came only a few months later, in July 1958, when Pombo and others took part in the battles that turned back the Batista regime's final military offensive aimed at defeating the guerrillas in the Sierra. Then, in early September, Villegas joined the westward march of Rebel

---

3. José Martí (1853–1895), noted poet, writer, speaker, and journalist, founded the Cuban Revolutionary Party to fight Spanish rule and oppose U.S. designs on Cuba. He launched the 1895 independence war and was killed in battle. His revolutionary anti-imperialist program is part of the international political heritage of the Cuban revolution.

Army Column no. 8, under Guevara's command, that culminated in the New Year's victory over government forces in Santa Clara, Cuba's third-largest city, and the nationwide general strike and triumphant revolutionary insurrection the first week of January 1959.

The Bolivia campaign

We turned to a discussion of the guerrilla struggle in Bolivia where Pombo accompanied Che nearly a decade later. For eleven months, until he was wounded, captured, and executed by CIA-organized military forces in October 1967, Guevara led a group of some forty combatants in Bolivia, attempting to forge the nucleus of a revolutionary movement that could bring down the military dictatorship in Bolivia and open the road to deepening anticapitalist struggle across Latin America.

Throughout this entire campaign, Pombo was one of its central cadres.

In Bolivia, too, Villegas commented, Che never stopped pressing those he worked with and led to study and broaden their cultural horizons. The combatants in Bolivia developed a library of more than 300 books and established a system whereby each person carried a few of them in his knapsack, read them, and then passed them on to another fighter.[4]

"For Che, raising the cultural level of the combatants was a constant," Pombo explained. "Che saw the combatants as future leaders and viewed the guerrilla unit as a school for forging revolutionaries and leaders. Being part of a social environment where abject poverty prevails, as it does among the peasantry, allows one to acquire a deeper awareness of the need for revolutionary change, to become more human, more humanistic, more conscious of the need to transform society. Out of that kind of experience come men who can be counted on politically, and that is the foundation.

---

4. For more on political education within the guerrilla unit in Bolivia, see the account by Pombo titled "On the Guerrillas' Battle for Culture," in *The Bolivian Diary of Ernesto Che Guevara*, pp. 426–28.

Initiation of the armed insurrection against the U.S.-backed Batista dictatorship had a big impact on young people throughout Cuba, says Harry Villegas, who joined the Rebel Army when he was 17.

Top: Fidel Castro, who commanded the Rebel Army, addresses peasants in the Sierra Maestra, early 1958. *Bottom:* Ernesto Che Guevara with members of his column following liberation of city of Fomento, December 1958, as the revolutionary victory over Batista dictatorship neared. From left: Hermes Peña, Mongo Martínez, Guevara, Jesús Parra, Sobeida Rodríguez, Víctor Bordón, and José Ramón Silva.

"Che looked for men and women who are made of good timber. Then, as Fidel says, the wood can be shaped. Leaders who are forged in adverse conditions develop a deep sense of fraternity, of comradeship, knowing that human beings need each other, cannot live as hermits like Robinson Crusoe. In order to withstand the hostile environment of the Sierra, to really be able to fight, one has to be part of a collective effort. In such a context human qualities are born, allowing future leaders to be forged."

There is no necessary contradiction between comradeship and friendship, Villegas added. We can take Martí as our guide in this too. For Martí, "comradeship exists between human beings who are fighting for the same cause, who are fighting for the same objective. But within this bond there is also Martí's concept of friendship as presented in his 'Simple Verses,' where he says, 'The president has a treasure of gold and wheat, but I have something more, I have a friend. The leopard has a shelter, but in the forest I have more than the leopard, because I have a friend.'[5]

"Friendship is a *feeling* that develops through human contact."

Che sought to instill these human qualities in future leaders, Pombo emphasized, "And part of this process was precisely encouraging them to raise their educational and cultural level. For this he created a school. Wherever Che went, there was a school; there was a school in Africa, a school in Bolivia, a school in the Sierra Maestra, a school in Las Villas. Wherever Che began a campaign, alongside it came instruction, education."

"The study of mathematics was also obligatory," Pombo continued. Che considered it the basis for mastering any science.

5. "The leopard has a shelter / in his forest brown and dry: / I have more than the leopard, / Because I have a good friend. . . . / The president has / a garden with a fountain, / and a treasure of gold and wheat: / I have more; I have a friend." Translated from José Martí, "Versos sencillos" in *Obras completas*, vol. 16 (Havana: Editorial de Ciencias Sociales, 1975), p. 122.

"And even while we were still in the Sierra, Che taught us the art of irregular warfare. We read Clausewitz's *On War* and discussed it. We read Mao Zedong on guerrilla warfare.[6] Che was preparing himself through self-education, as well as teaching us."

Later, Villegas noted, when Che wrote his own book, *Guerrilla Warfare,* published in Cuba in 1960, "the North Americans used it as a textbook to prepare their special forces to confront the guerrilla movements in Latin America. They considered it the most finished document on irregular warfare from the military point of view, the most practical, the most objective."

Land, peasants, and revolution

In Bolivia the Cuban internationalist volunteers "confronted a world very different from our own," Pombo observed, even though both countries are part of Latin America. "Cuba is an island, where virtually no indigenous population survived. The Spaniards exterminated them. We had no idea of the life of the Indian, of their psychology. We tried to learn about it by reading novels dealing with everyday life."

Guevara was closer to the local population in Bolivia, Villegas noted, because he himself was from that part of the world. "Che had lived side by side with the indigenous people, and he was able to transmit some of his understanding to us."

"Che had gone through an important experience in Africa too," Pombo continued, referring to the six months Guevara spent during 1965 helping to advance the national liberation struggle in the Congo. "It is not easy to assimilate

6. Karl von Clausewitz (1780–1831) was a Prussian general who served under both the Prussian and Russian monarchies in the wars against Napoleon. He was the author of *On War,* long considered a classic of military strategy.

Mao Zedong, the central leader of the Chinese Communist Party from the mid-1930s until his death in 1976, was the author of numerous articles on guerrilla warfare and other military writings used by the People's Liberation Army that triumphed over the landlord-capitalist regime of Chiang Kai-shek in the Chinese revolution of 1949.

a culture overnight," he said. "One must have a grounding. It requires a broadly cultured person, someone capable of assimilating that culture without being assimilated by it. Che became very conscious of this in Africa."

"In Bolivia he struggled to have us understand the indigenous people's world view, their life, traditions, and rich history. Despite having lived through a revolution in Cuba, we did not have this understanding."

Che had "studied the combative traditions of the Bolivians, their history of struggles," Pombo said. "He went looking for it, and this was one of the things he explained to us. Che knew the characteristics of the Indians, in the same way he knew the peasants in Cuba.

"Peasants are conservative," Pombo continued. "In the Sierra, despite all the work that had been done by Celia [Sánchez][7] who had already recruited peasants and organized them into a cell of the movement, this was true. The peasant is not inclined to support a movement until he sees possibilities of success in that movement. This is even more true when the movement is not completely an agrarian one" — as the July 26 Movement was not; most of its initial cadres and leaders were from cities or small towns.

"When it is an agrarian movement, in which the peasant is defending his little plot of land, he develops somewhat more rapidly. Che knew this," Villegas said. "This was what he explained to us." It was to advance this process that Che paid special attention to the leadership development of the Bolivian combatants.

Bolivia and Vietnam

In Bolivia, as earlier in Cuba, Che's goal was to bring all the diverse forces together in action to overthrow the Bolivian dictatorship and advance the struggle against imperialist domination throughout the entire region.

7. Celia Sánchez (1920–1980) was a founding leader of the July 26 Movement in Oriente Province and the first woman combatant in the Rebel Army.

"The foundations of the National Liberation Army of Bolivia were very broad," Pombo noted. Che never conceived of the war in a sectarian manner. He worked primarily with the Communist Party; it was our job to work with them. But he also worked with the factions within the Communist Party. He called on the party of Juan Lechín for support.[8] He worked with all the organizations that supported Bolivia's freedom. He always worked for the participation of all honest people, all revolutionaries, everyone who wanted to fight for independence, for the liberation of Latin America — because his conception in Bolivia involved not only Bolivia, but Latin America."

It is necessary to remember what was happening in Latin America and the world at the time Che decided to go to Bolivia, Pombo continued. "As combatants we studied the world situation that Che evaluates in his 'Message to the Tricontinental.'[9] That was part of the school, the training of future leaders. Above all, the world situation was marked by the genocidal war being waged against the people of Vietnam."

"The war in Vietnam, as you know better than we do, shook the world. It shook U.S. society — the Vietnam syndrome, the economic crisis generated by the war and from which imperialism has never completely recovered.

"Che was a man who analyzed things deeply. He was convinced that it was necessary to take advantage of that conjuncture to inflict defeats on imperialism, to take advantage of the war's political and economic impact. That was the most effective way to assist the heroic people of Vietnam. Out of these considerations came the call contained in the message Che sent to the Tricontinental to create 'two, three, many Vietnams,' right here on the doorstep of U.S. imperialism. The peoples of Latin America were the ones

8. Juan Lechín was the central leader of the Bolivian trade union federation. He organized the Revolutionary Party of the National Left in 1964.
9. Guevara's article is included in *Pombo: A Man of Che's guerrilla,* and in *Che Guevara Speaks,* published by Pathfinder.

who had already taken the first step."

Throughout Latin America, Pombo explained, there were guerrilla movements fighting in Venezuela, in Colombia, Guatemala, Peru. "It was a propitious moment. Vietnam was the center, but revolutionary movements were flowering throughout the world; other forces too were standing up to oppression. Che was aware of this, and that is how he developed the strategy he elaborated in the 'Message to the Tricontinental.' "

This was not just Che's evaluation, however, Villegas stressed. "In all honesty, we must say that the Cuban revolution supported this course entirely. This is what Fidel was teaching too. Remember what Che said in his letter to Fidel: that he was leaving to do 'that which is denied you owing to your responsibility at the head of Cuba.'[10] Che was completely convinced that Fidel would have been the first to go, had he been able. And for this reason we also participated. We had Cuban comrades in Venezuela at the time; others were in Guatemala, or on their way to Colombia. The Cuban revolution gave support to all these movements that sought liberation for the world's hungry masses."

In launching the Bolivian campaign, Villegas said, Guevara was "looking for an integration of the peoples, not only of revolutionaries, not only of honest people as individuals, but of nations that truly need to achieve their independence in all regards — economically and socially. There were Peruvians, Argentines, Bolivians, and Cubans fighting together, shoulder to shoulder.

"The idea of Latin American unity is not an idea dreamed up by Che; it is an idea with a history. It has a basis in the history of struggle of our America. It was the program of Simón Bolívar and José Martí that Che was trying to make a reality because the question of unity has never been resolved. To be strong and equal with the other America, the integration of the Latin American peoples is needed."

10. Guevara's 1965 letter to Fidel Castro, written right before he left Cuba, is published in the *Bolivian Diary*, pp. 71–73, and in *Che Guevara Speaks*.

"Martí's program for Latin America," Villegas explained, "has never been achieved, and this is not only a question of unity. In his writings, Martí says: 'Create a republic where the first law will be respect for the dignity of man.' This cannot be achieved under capitalism. He was thinking of a different society. And when he says: 'This is a republic including all and for the welfare of all,' he is talking of a more universal republic, where men are truly equal in rights, in possibilities, and this can be achieved only under socialism.

"In other words, one of the things Che discovered through his study of Cuba's history is that the goals of Martí converge with the course of Marxism-Leninism. This is true even with regard to the party, and the conception of how to lead, how to conduct the struggle. Martí's ideas are not at all separate from the conceptions of Marxism.

"This is an indigenous part of Cuba's history, an extraordinarily profound phenomenon. That is what gives us greater strength.

"That is why today we can say that all our political work must deepen patriotism," Villegas added. Not nationalism, but patriotism, a pride in our history of struggle. "Because patriotism has very deep roots in Martí, and we can go back even further, to Céspedes, to Maceo.[11] Martí fought hard for unity between the veterans of the war of 1868 and the 'new pines,' as he called the next generation.

"All this is part of Martí's body of ideas, and you can see how it has been put into practice by Fidel, and how Che was totally connected with it. We can say that, in a real sense, drawing on this body of ideas, Che matures in Cuba."

To construct the republic that Martí "dreamed about," Pombo said, "it could be nothing but a socialist republic — one without exploitation, without inequalities. There would be no other way, and this is part of our roots, of our history,

11. Carlos Manuel de Céspedes was the central leader of the Cuban independence war launched in 1868; he was ambushed by Spanish troops and killed in 1874. Antonio Maceo was a military leader of both independence wars who was killed in battle in 1896.

of our own conceptions. . . . That is why we always say, 'What Martí promised, Fidel carried out.' That is the truth."

Revolutionary upheaval in Southern Cone

Che's military plan in Bolivia aimed at achieving an element of strategic surprise, Pombo noted, by launching a guerrilla struggle where U.S. imperialism was least prepared.

Strategic surprise, Villegas explained, is different from tactical surprise. The U.S. forces attacking Iraq in 1991, he noted, based their military plan on their firepower and numerical superiority. "They could afford to say, 'We are going to attack Iraq' and begin to prepare, to assemble their forces openly six months in advance. There was no strategic surprise, even though they could have achieved a tactical surprise. No one knew the moment when the war was to be unleashed."

"But Che wanted strategic surprise. Why? Because with the flowering of revolutionary struggles throughout Latin America in the wake of imperialism's defeat in Cuba, the North American government had spent millions looking for a way to respond. They established the Alliance for Progress in the economic sphere, and in the military realm they gave massive assistance with their Green Berets, creating powerful counterinsurgency forces. No one knows how much the Pentagon and the CIA spent to defeat the revolutionary movements in Latin America."

"But the imperialists were not expecting the rise of a guerrilla movement in Bolivia. They considered it impossible, as did the Bolivian generals at that time, because they thought there had already been a revolution in Bolivia. That is how they looked at the revolt of 1952."[12]

12. A powerful mass upsurge in Bolivia in 1952 resulted in nationalization of the largest tin mines, legalization of the trade unions, initiation of land reform, and the elimination of the literacy requirement that had effectively disenfranchised the majority of Bolivia's people, the Aymará- and Quechua-speaking population. But Bolivia remained one of the most impoverished countries of the Americas. The increasingly corrupt and fractured government of the Revolutionary Nationalist Movement (MNR), a bourgeois party that initially had

Che, however, had traveled through Bolivia in 1953, Pombo noted, and "he knew that this revolution had begun to deteriorate from the moment of its birth. He knew that the needs of the peasantry, of the miners, of the poor, had not been met. That the agrarian reform had never had any technical assistance, any economic backing. He knew that [Victor] Paz Estenssoro, the leader of the MNR, the Revolutionary Nationalist Movement, was not a real revolutionary. He was not a man of the people."

Che with his typically biting humor called the Bolivian revolution of 1952 the "DDT revolution," Pombo remarked, because "before Paz Estenssoro would meet with an Indian, with a worker, he would have the person fumigated so they could not infect him with any diseases."

Washington and the Pentagon didn't understand any of this, however, Villegas said. "They thought there could not be a revolution where there had been a revolution. Che's military plan was unquestionably well conceived. It was a total surprise. They had to scurry to get the counterinsurgency troops prepared."

Che's plan assumed, as a condition for success, the participation and support of the Bolivian Communist Party, Pombo noted. But the commitments made by that party's general secretary, Mario Monje, were never fulfilled. The guerrilla forces were annihilated before they could reach the area they intended to operate from and establish lines of communication and supply. Yet, politically, Che's assessment of the social explosion building in Bolivia was accurate. A profound new revolutionary upsurge did occur in Bolivia — and elsewhere in Latin America's Southern Cone — in the years just following the movement's defeat.

"Imagine if things had gone as planned," Pombo remarked, "if a general uprising had occurred when the guerrillas were already operating in their zones, and had

strong support from Bolivia's superexploited tin miners, was overthrown by a military coup in 1964.

19

been able to incorporate new forces. If that had happened, it would not have taken long to seize power in Bolivia.

"And after taking power, to defend their revolution the Bolivian masses would have been compelled to come to the aid of revolutionary struggles in surrounding countries. They would have had to do so to survive, because Bolivia is a landlocked country, and this was another element in Che's thinking. Bolivia is a *mediterranean* country, one without access to the sea — which is not the way the term *mediterranean* is used in other parts of the world to signify a sea surrounded by land."[13]

This fact of Bolivia's geographical location, Pombo said, "was involved from the beginning in Che's strategy. Che was convinced the U.S. forces would become involved in the attempt to destroy the revolutionary movement. In fact, the objective was to draw them in.

"But first we had to take an area and then establish political power in a country. The point was not to begin everything at the same time, but to begin in one place and extend outward to other areas. The Peruvians fighting with us would go to Peru, and so forth. Che's aim was to develop political and military leaders among the Bolivians and others. He saw Inti [Peredo] as a man with extraordinary potential to lead the entire movement, for example. He noted that Coco [Peredo] was beginning to show signs of military leadership."[14]

Che rarely talked about the Cuban cadres in his *Diary*, Pombo recalled, because "he took it for granted that we were there to play the role of a catalyst, to transmit experiences and knowledge." The composition of the general staff of the Bolivian campaign is important. "Notice the assignments Che made: how there was a political officer to attend

13. The Spanish word *mediterráneo*, which means "landlocked," is also, as in many other languages, the name of the sea surrounded by the coasts of northern Africa, southern Europe, and the Middle East.
14. Inti Peredo's account of the Bolivian campaign, *My Campaign with Che*, is included in the Pathfinder edition of *The Bolivian Diary*.

to the Cubans, but also a political officer for the Bolivians.[15] This was the integration he conceived of. In other words, his aim was not to lead the Bolivians. His aim was to coordinate the whole movement in the Southern Cone. That was his aim.

"Sooner or later," Pombo said, "Che aimed to go to Argentina. He considered himself an Argentine."

Had Washington eventually been drawn in and intervened with its own forces, Villegas explained, "they would have had to establish overland supply lines that would have been extremely vulnerable. If they entered through Argentina, for example, they would have been unable to protect their supply lines without an enormous investment of men. In this way alone, we would have already achieved an objective: they eventually would have had to send in even more troops than went to Vietnam.

"The North American people would not have put up with that. The U.S. military, even today, does not want to fight anywhere their troops would be at risk. They need technical superiority, with maximum assurance that there will be no deaths. That is a legacy of Vietnam.

"But while they might have a high level of technology, they have not been able to invent anything to destroy homemade weapons — like a Vietnamese trap, where a man simply falls into a hole and is buried. What can they invent to use against a man in hiding, who resists for days? Against a man who, when the enemy comes in to get him, has laid a mine for them?

"Against a man who is willing to give his life, they have not been able to find an answer in technology — nor will they ever.

15. As a member of the general staff, Inti Peredo was one of two officers assigned as a political commissar of the unit, responsible for political leadership of the combatants. The other was Eliseo Reyes (*Rolando*), a veteran of Che's column in the Rebel Army and previously a member of the Central Committee of the Communist Party of Cuba who volunteered for the internationalist mission in Bolivia and was killed in combat in April 1967.

With the January 1, 1959, victory workers, peasants, and youth began transforming the whole of society as they transformed themselves.

Top: Peasant receives title to land after first agrarian reform, 1959. *Above:* Youth teaches fishing boat crew in Surgidero de Batabanó during 1961 literacy drive. *Opposite page top:* Che Guevara in Holguín, Cuba, addresses rally celebrating the transformation of the dictatorship's former military garrison into a school, February 1960. *Bottom:* Workers mobilize to carry out expropriation of U.S. banks, September 1960.

"This is the conviction that guides our concept of the war of the entire people here in Cuba today.[16] Che was very clear on this; he had thought about it deeply."

Angola and Cuban internationalism

Recalling Fidel Castro's reaffirmation in December 1988 that "whoever is incapable of fighting for others will never be capable of fighting for himself,"[17] we asked Villegas to return to the question of internationalism, of Guevara's example, and the contribution of the Cuban revolution in helping to bring down the apartheid regime in South Africa.

From 1975 to 1989 nearly half a million Cuban volunteers took part in internationalist missions in the former Portuguese colony of Angola. They were responding to the request from the newly independent government there to help defeat the invading troops of South Africa and Zaire and the rightist Angolan forces led by Jonas Savimbi, which were financed and aided not only by the apartheid regime but by Washington as well.

The defeat of the South African armed forces and their allies at the historic battle of Cuito Cuanavale in early 1988 — a battle in which Villegas participated — was a decisive turning point in the history of all southern Africa. It led to negotiations later that year involving the Cuban, South African, and U.S. governments that opened the door to ending the civil war in Angola; achieving independence for the South African–controlled territory of Namibia; and bringing Cuba's internationalist mission in Angola to a close. The victory at Cuito Cuanavale gave a powerful boost

16. The "war of the entire people" is the name by which the defense strategy of the Cuban revolution is popularly known there. Millions of Cubans have been trained to fight and have an assigned post to report for duty in case of imperialist aggression.
17. From Fidel Castro's December 5, 1988, speech, "As Long as the Empire Exists, We Will Never Lower Our Guard," in Pathfinder's *In Defense of Socialism: Four Speeches on the 30th Anniversary of the Cuban Revolution*, p. 28.

to the mass antiapartheid struggle in South Africa as well.[18]

The internationalist aid to Angola over a thirteen-year period was an enormous effort for a relatively small and economically underdeveloped nation such as Cuba. Beginning in 1989, almost simultaneous with the end of the Angolan mission, the disintegration of the Eastern European and Soviet regimes led to the collapse of most of Cuba's foreign trade agreements and many aid projects. Amid the severe economic crisis that has marked Cuba for the last half decade, it has not been unusual to hear some Cubans express the view that the resources that went to help Angola would have been better utilized at home.

We asked Villegas, who spent most of his life from 1981 to 1990 in Angola, for his opinion.

"Cuba's aid to Angola was not only worthwhile," he replied, "but if we were capable of doing it again, we would do so.

"More than half a million Cubans carried out internationalist missions in Africa, between Angola and Ethiopia[19] and elsewhere — some 375,000 military personnel, plus those who went as public health workers, to teach, and to do other work. It is a large number. We can say that Cuba is a nation of internationalists. And when one speaks of internationalism in Cuba, what people see is Che. That is, Che's example opened up for us a broader concept of internationalism.

"Fidel said that when we go to Africa, we go to pay our

18. For further information on the Cuban mission in Angola and its international impact, see the July 1991 speeches of Nelson Mandela and Fidel Castro, published in Pathfinder's *How Far We Slaves Have Come!*

19. In 1977, Cuba responded to a request by the government of Ethiopia to help defeat a U.S.-backed invasion by the regime in neighboring Somalia aimed at seizing the Ogaden region. Washington planned to use a Somalian victory as a springboard to help turn back land redistribution and other measures that had been taken in Ethiopia following the overthrow of the landlord-based monarchy of Emperor Haile Selassie in 1974.

debt to the African peoples. And in large measure that is true. But I think that the justice of the sacrifice — of the effort made in Angola, in particular — has borne fruit. Why is this so?

"In the first place, do you believe we could be speaking today of a South Africa led by Nelson Mandela had it not been for this effort? That the Black majority of 75 percent or 85 percent would be in power? Do you think that if the South Africans had not been defeated militarily and economically, apartheid would have been eliminated? If we did nothing more than indirectly help defeat apartheid, our effort was unquestionably worthwhile.

"Millions of human beings have been given the possibility to realize their human potential. This is why Che fought, why all progressive humanity has fought, why men and women of dignity have fought everywhere. This is what Fidel is fighting for. This is why the Cuban people resist.

"And that battle was won. Not only do we see what has been conquered in South Africa, we also see the independence of Namibia that has been established, and the right of the African peoples there to speak as full human beings. In the case of Angola, independence was achieved, with whatever qualifications, and it could not have been realized any other way. Perhaps it was a dream of ours to think that socialism could be built in Angola. But South Africa was prevented from dominating Angola; its aim of carving up Angola, in connivance with the regime in Zaire, could not be carried out.

"For these reasons, I am totally convinced that there is no work of greater value than the internationalism of Cuba in Africa, and not only in Africa, in Latin America too. Whether or not the final objectives were achieved, these are glorious pages in the history of the peoples that have created the foundations for the future."

I have done
what is normal
for a
revolutionary

Interview by
Elsa Blaquier Ascaño

I still remember him as extremely thin, with an almost beardless face and fine features contrasting against the darkness of his skin, all of which gave him an appearance even younger than his twenty-five years. It took a real effort to see in him the battle-tested veteran of the guerrilla struggle in the Sierra Maestra, the western invasion, the taking of Santa Clara, and the internationalist aid to the Congo.

Then, without a moment's rest, he again undertook an important mission together with the man who had taken him in as a seventeen-year-old soldier and to whom he was united with ties that not even death could break: Che.

In those days of May 1965, together with José María Martínez Tamayo (Papi) and Carlos Coello (Tuma), he was preparing the logistical and organizational foundations for what was to become the Bolivian guerrilla movement.

Today a brigadier general, Harry Villegas Tamayo has

This interview was originally published in the June 12, 1995, issue of *Trabajadores,* the weekly newspaper of the Central Organization of Cuban Workers. Elsa Blaquier Ascaño is a veteran Cuban journalist who writes for the National News Agency (AIN). She is also the widow of René Martínez Tamayo (*Arturo*), a Cuban revolutionary fighter killed in Bolivia with Guevara.

27

since added new pages to his record as an internationalist and as a military leader, which earn him the right to wear on his chest the gold star of Hero of the Republic of Cuba, which the Council of State recently awarded him.

Harry continues being Pombo, whom the Cuban people met through Che's *Bolivian Diary;* the one who amazed the world with the feat of commanding the small group that was able to elude their encirclement by the CIA after the death of the Heroic Guerrilla.

His modesty has caused him to avoid interviews other than those where he speaks of his unforgettable leader and teacher. Today, however, he was unable to escape the siege and we made him remember his childhood in Yara, at the entrance to the eastern mountains. He recalled how his father Andrés, a carpenter, taught him a sense of justice and humanity, and how his mother Engracia, a housewife with a great gift for commerce, instilled in him her talent in business matters.

He was born near the Sierra Maestra on May 10, 1940, and was influenced by the traditions of those parts. Near there is the tamarind tree where it is said that Hatuey was burned at the stake,[1] and very near the spot where Céspedes freed his slaves and issued the first call for Cuba's independence. He was like all the young boys there, a good baseball player and an enthusiastic swimmer in the nearby river.

"I was the tenth and youngest child; I was able to study because my mother had come by some money from two stores and a bakery that she had in Yara and Palma. My father, on the other hand, had nothing; he was very generous and used to give everything away.

Che for the first time

"When the struggle in the Sierra Maestra began, I was studying commerce in Manzanillo. That event had a deep im-

---

1. Hatuey, a Taino Indian chief, led an uprising against the Spaniards; he was captured and executed in 1511.

pact on me, and I immediately joined the underground movement. After several jailings inside the rural guard's garrison, I decided to join the rebels, although my mother was opposed because she felt I was too skinny and couldn't take it."

Pombo first joined a group of men in the Cauto valley armed with hunting rifles. Later he made contact with Chino Figueredo's troops, and was with them when Che arrived. He remembers the great impression made on him that day by this guerrilla fighter, who was already a symbol.

"He asked what we were doing there, who had sent us. We said we were there to fight for Cuba's freedom and that it had been our own decision. He then told us to go down to the plains and disarm some soldiers so that each of us could return with a weapon."

Although the undertaking turned out to be difficult, they did not return empty-handed. Che allowed them to stay, more for the determination they had shown than for the quality of the weapons they had captured.

"I began as a messenger. Later I went with him to the school at Minas del Frío, where I had to accustom myself to constant bombing by Batista's planes, which had become a trial-by-fire for the rebel troops."

There he received the first demonstration of his leader's high standard of discipline. "The food here was not the worst, but there wasn't much. A comrade named Lorente began a hunger strike and I was among the leaders.

"When Che arrived he accused us of sedition and threatened to shoot whoever was responsible. I was punished with three days without eating; the others were ordered to stand at attention all day, in spite of the air attacks.

"Luckily Fidel came and spoke to him, and he then softened the punishment. Che knew that discipline was a decisive factor for a guerrilla unit's survival. Moreover, it began with the harsh discipline he imposed on himself. He struggled with us as if we were his children, trying to educate and train us in every sense, and to criticize and punish us when necessary."

Turning back the offensive of the tyranny was Pombo's

first great combat mission, together with Leonardo Tamayo, Pablo Ribalta, and Hermes Peña — the same individuals who later became the Heroic Guerrilla's personal escort. "We were selected to participate in the battle of El Jigüe and later in the encirclement to prevent Batista's army from reaching the command post at La Plata.

"The majority of us were just kids: San Luis, Joel Iglesias, Tamayo, Hermes Peña, Carlos Coello (Tuma).[2] Che's command post platoon, where I was assigned, was a school; we studied mathematics, Spanish, tactics, guerrilla warfare; we read novels and history books. I wasn't among those who progressed the most, so Che used to tell me that I was an intellectual who had graduated from "Yara University." He liked to surround himself with youth and force us to improve ourselves."

The battles of Cuatro Compañeros and La Federal, occurring on the plains during the invasion, the historic march toward Villa Clara, are etched in his memory. So too are Che's efforts to unite the revolutionary forces that operated in the Escambray mountains, among them the Second Front, which opposed having the July 26 Movement operate there.[3]

"The Las Villas campaign can be considered as a lightning operation; in it Che graduated as a strategist and consolidated his abilities as a military leader," Pombo says, adding, "He went against the laws of warfare that call for numerical superiority before launching an attack.

"He calculated that surprise was a psychological factor

2. San Luis (Eliseo Reyes) fought with Guevara in Bolivia, under the name of "Rolando"; he was killed in April 1967. Joel Iglesias was a leader of Guevara's column in Cuba's revolutionary war. Leonard Tamayo (Urbano) served with Guevara in Bolivia and was one of the three Cuban combatants to fight their way out. Hermes Peña was killed in Argentina in 1964, supporting a guerrilla effort in the Salta mountains. Carlos Coello (Tuma) was killed in Bolivia in June 1967.
3. For more information on the campaign in Las Villas province (today Villa Clara) and the Second National Front of the Escambray, see Guevara's *Episodes of the Cuban Revolutionary War 1956–58* (Pathfinder, 1996), pp. 323–40 and 360–98.

that weakened the 3,000 soldiers defending Santa Clara, while we numbered about 300. Che had a daring recklessness, but he wouldn't just give his life away. In that battle he proved very audacious. He was the first to enter the city, accompanied only by Aleida, Parra, and me.[4] As we advanced, people came out and said: 'Here comes Che with some women!' because we had long hair.

"Havana scared me. When we arrived at the La Cabaña military fortress, I looked at it from atop the statue of Christ and I didn't dare go out until the day Che arrived and asked me if I, the head of his personal escort, intended to go around doing nothing. That's how I found out about my assignment. I got in the car with him and finally left."

As a member of the escort, Pombo lived for many years together with Che and his family, until starting a family of his own. He was given the responsibility of attending the school of administration, of directing several enterprises, later returning to the Revolutionary Armed Forces.

"By then I had a son, Harry Andrés, and I had carried out several military and political responsibilities. For some time I had not seen Che because he was traveling and I was serving in the tank unit of Managua, until one day they came to look for me. I spent several days together with Carlos Coello on a farm in Cubanacán, and Tuma said to me, jokingly, "So much eating without working will lead to no good.""

Fidel gave us the mission to see that nothing happened to Che

"Fidel sent for us and said that Che had selected us to accompany him, that he was already in Africa responding to a request for help from the revolutionary movement that de-

---

4. Aleida March, later Guevara's wife, was a member of the July 26 Movement underground in Cienfuegos and Las Villas, often serving as a courier; she remained with Rebel Army after the Batista's forces discovered her identity in late 1958. Jesús Parra was a member of Guevara's personal escort.

veloped after the death of Lumumba,[5] and he gave us the mission of helping Che and guaranteeing that nothing happened to him. It was a proof of trust, which moved us deeply.

"That's how we ended up in Cairo after passing through several countries, and from there to Dar es Salaam, the capital of Tanzania. Upon arriving we joined up with the group that was preparing to enter Congo (Leopoldville), later Zaire. Che, Papi, and Víctor Dreke were already in the Congo.[6] About three days after arriving at the camp, we left. Pablo Ribalta, who was ambassador to Tanzania, explained the situation to us. We crossed the country in an area of nature reserve parks and arrived at Lake Tanganyika; it was impressive, with its 35,000 square kilometers of fresh water, where the wind stirred up enormous waves.

"We crossed in a canoe. On the other side we found a hut; inside it was a Cuban doctor (Kumy), who gave me a backpack that weighed about 75 pounds. I had not trained like the other comrades, so when I began to climb that mountain more than 1,700 meters high with that weight on my back, I had to ask for help. Then Tuma said to me: 'I told you, so much eating without working would lead to no good.'

"Che made me head of services (supplies, medicine, transportation) and assigned me to the same cabin he was

5. Patrice Lumumba, central leader of the independence movement in the former Belgian colony of the Congo, and its first prime minister, was murdered in January 1961 by imperialist-backed forces loyal to rightist figure Moise Tshombe. Lumumba had been under the "protection" of United Nations troops.

   In mid-1964, a new revolt broke out in the Congo led by forces that supported Lumumba. They were defeated in November 1964 with the help of Belgian and South African mercenary armies — politically and militarily backed by Washington — whose assignment was to prevent the vast mineral wealth of the Congo from escaping imperialist control. Thousands of Congolese were massacred.

6. Papi (José María Martínez) served with Che in the Congo and later in Bolivia; Víctor Dreke was second in command of Cuban forces in the Congo.

living in. Chino, a member of his personal escort, was there too, as was a Congolese guerrilla fighter named Ernesto, who spoke French and taught Che Swahili. As one could imagine, I had to join in the classes."

The struggle in the Congo was a great experience

"The Congo was a great experience for everyone. It was very difficult to understand the psychology of the African commanders, most of whom were not there. We kept waiting for an African leader until Che decided to begin fighting the Belgian and South African mercenaries. It turned out to be a complex affair to understand the people there, who were living under a mixture of social stages, from the familial relations of the primitive community to more modern displays such as walking around with small portable radios or big wrist watches.

"We fought several important battles, like the one at Force Bandera where we lost Vinajera, Pío, Ballester, Warner Moro, and fourteen Rwandans. We attacked and took the posts at Mwenga and Kovimvira, conducted several ambushes along the road to the lake, and led a surprise attack on the river port. There was real combat, and it was done with effectiveness, but the whole question of the leadership on the part of the Congolese created instability.

"At one point Che thought about going to the other end of the country to look for other groups that were fighting, but it would have involved a march of thousands of kilometers. As this was being considered, the meeting of African heads of state took place. They decided to alter the character of the assistance being given to the revolutionary movement in the Congo, allowing armed cooperation only with the independence movements of the Portuguese colonies — which was also within Che's conception of the struggle.[7]

"The contribution that he was making there was really a pause before going to South America, and in particular Ar-

---

7. Meeting in Accra, Ghana, October 21–26, 1965, the Organization of African Unity decided to limit military aid by foreign powers.

gentina. But he did not want to leave there without having the request for our departure put in writing, to keep Cuba's prestige unblemished. It was also painful for us to leave behind the more than three thousand African fighters who were accompanying us.

"From a human standpoint, that situation was very difficult for Che, and I know it was very hard for him to accept abandoning the struggle. Che spoke with them and asked them to choose twenty fighters to return with us to Cuba — it couldn't be more, because the boats had only enough room to carry the hundred or so Cubans who found ourselves there."

Out of that epic endeavor Harry kept the nickname of Pombo, part of the pseudonym his commander had given him: Pombo Pojo, which in the native language means green nectar. His eyes betray the happiness he felt when the unforgettable guerrilla met with Papi, Tuma, and him to ask if they would be willing to follow him to another part of the world.

From Africa to South America

"We immediately said yes. When we arrived at Dar es Salaam we left the other Cubans and traveled in pairs to Prague. There we remained for a long time preparing for the new mission, until Fidel convinced him to return to Cuba.

"Papi was already in La Paz, making contact with the leadership of the Bolivian Communist Party; Tuma and I also went. We were charged with providing cover to Papi in all the organizational arrangements; then we were in Cuba for a few days.

"In July 1966 we departed for Bolivia, passing through many countries on the way. We planned out the arrival of all the comrades, looked for and bought the farm, discussed with Mario Monje having the [Bolivian Communist] Party join the struggle. We were involved in this until November 3, when Che arrived."

The confidence that Pombo's commander placed in him can be seen on every page of his diary written on Bolivian soil; Pombo was once again named head of services and was included on the general staff. There are countless references to Pombo being chosen to lead a scouting party or to evaluate where to set up camp.

On June 26, 1967, Che writes: "A black day for me. . . . We received word of two wounded: Pombo in the leg and Tuma in the stomach. . . . Pombo's wound is superficial . . . Tuma . . . died during the operation. With his death I have lost an inseparable comrade and companion over all the recent years. His loyalty was unwavering, and I feel his absence almost as if he were my own son."[8]

Harry remembers the day he was wounded while trying to help his comrade of many battles and adventures. He recalls the events of October 8 with an equal measure of pain.[9]

"We were close to the crest of the hill. Che knew the army was there and organized the defense. He ordered Tamayo (Urbano) and me to fight along the lower part of the ravine. Our mission was to hold our position if the attack came from that direction so people could regroup and retreat, especially the sick, to a previously designated place.

"A moment before the firing began, Che sent the Bolivians Ñato and Aniceto to relieve us. Then the bullets began flying over us, we began to repel the attack, and we sent them to find out whether or not we were to leave. On their way back to our positions Aniceto was mortally wounded. Ñato told us that Che had already withdrawn.

"We tried to withdraw but the enemy fire did not allow it. Around 1:30 the shots began to grow more distant. It was evident they wanted to circle around to prevent Che and the sick who were with him from escaping.

"When we were able to withdraw we went to the point where his command post had been, and we found he had taken the most valuable items; this indicated he was alive

8. Ernesto Che Guevara, *Bolivian Diary*, pp. 218–19.
9. Guevara was captured by Bolivian troops October 8. The following day he was executed on orders of Bolivian president René Barrientos, after consultation with Washington.

and was withdrawing to the agreed-upon location.

"We began climbing; when we were almost there they whistled, telling us not to move because we were surrounded. It was Dariel Alarcón (Benigno), Guido Peredo (Inti), and David Adriazola (Darío). We hit the ground and fell back to the ravine once again. About 6:00 P.M. the soldiers arrived again, threatening to lob grenades at us, but didn't. Later we regrouped. We continued moving all night long as the army harassed us.

"At dawn on October 9 we were hiding very close to the small schoolhouse at La Higuera. We saw the soldiers, observed the helicopters, but never imagined they were holding Che there. In the morning we heard the first news of his capture but reports were very confused, saying he was wounded, then saying he was not and that it was one of his officers. Finally they began to give details about his clothing and personal effects, and we knew it was true.

"It was a big blow, something terrible. We then decided to keep on fighting, that for us the war was not over, that we would fight together and nobody would be left behind. Inti, who was the political leader of the guerrilla unit remained as such, and I assumed command of the group."

Then came the search for the sick,[10] in whose defense Che had offered his precious life; the impossibility of finding them; breaking through one encirclement after another, which turned the march to the Chilean border into a feat truly fit for a novel, from which they came out alive thanks to the help of the revolutionary movement and the efforts of Salvador Allende, then a senator, who accompanied them back to the island.[11]

After arriving in Cuba he returned to the ranks of the armed forces as chief of operations of the Eastern Army

10. Four members of the guerrilla unit, most of them sick, had survived the battle of October 8 and fled in an opposite direction from Pombo's group. They were killed several days later.
11. Allende accompanied the guerrillas to Easter Island, a Chilean territory 2,300 miles off the coast, and then to Tahiti, in French territory, to assure their safety.

"I am convinced there is no work of greater value than the
internationalism of Cuba in Africa, in Latin America," says
Harry Villegas (Pombo).

Top: Villegas (at center left) during war in Angola that
turned back forces supported by imperialism and defeated
South Africa's apartheid army. *Inset:* Che Guevara, left,
and Pombo in Bolivia, late 1966 or early 1967.

Corps; he also participated in Operation Mambí, dedicated to preparing land for cultivation.[12] But he never abandoned hope of helping the revolutionaries renew the struggle in Bolivia. The death of Inti frustrated his plans.[13]

In Angola until the end of the internationalist mission

The artillery corps would have him as political leader; the "Máximo Gómez" Academy of the Revolutionary Armed Forces (FAR) would have him as one of its pupils; the Border Brigade at Guantánamo as its commander. Then came the request for assistance from the revolutionary movement for the liberation of Angola.

He went back and forth so many times it is impossible to give an accurate count. His long service record includes exploratory missions, operations against bandits in Cuando Cubango, the battles of Cangamba and Cuito Cuanavale. That is how his life was spent from 1981 to 1990, during which he remained permanently assigned in that country of Africa's southern cone until the total withdrawal of the Cuban internationalist troops.

He speaks nostalgically of the short amount of time he has been able to devote to his family and to his children: Harry Andrés, now 32 years old; Gabil Ernesto, 21; Pombo Alejandro, who has turned 13; and Yara Celia, the lovely eight-year-old.

He has just celebrated his fifty-fifth birthday and Brigadier General Harry Villegas Tamayo, now head of the political section of the Western Army, has built up a history that is hard to equal. Nevertheless, he declares that he does not feel himself to be a hero. "I believe I have done what is normal for a revolutionary. I always try to act with the loyalty and selfless dedication to humanity that Fidel and Che taught me since adolescence."

He is not old, he says. For him the struggle has not

12. Operation Mambí was part of the unsuccessful effort to harvest an unprecedented ten million tons of sugar in 1970.
13. Inti Peredo was killed by Bolivian army and police on September 9, 1969.

38

ended and he will continue defending the revolution and its immense accomplishments.

"To those who think the revolution was not worth it, I say that if they could see how much respect we have around the world, if they could feel what I have felt when I visit another country to talk about Che, they would realize that the world acknowledges that glory, which belongs to the entire Cuban people."

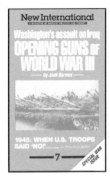

The Communist Manifesto

KARL MARX AND FREDERICK ENGELS

Founding document of the modern working-class movement, published in 1848. Explains why communists act on the basis not of preconceived principles but of *facts* springing from the actual class struggle, and why communism, to the degree it is a theory, is the generalization of the historical line of march of the working class and of the political conditions for its liberation. Also available in Spanish. $3.95

The History of the Russian Revolution

LEON TROTSKY

The social, economic, and political dynamics of the first socialist revolution. The story is told by one of the principal leaders of this victorious struggle for workers power headed by the Bolshevik party. Unabridged. $35.95

Teamster Rebellion

FARRELL DOBBS

The 1934 strikes that built an industrial union and a fighting social movement in Minneapolis, recounted by a central leader of that battle. The first in a four-volume series on the Teamster-led strikes and organizing drives in the Midwest that helped pave the way for the CIO and pointed a road toward independent labor political action. $16.95

How Far We Slaves Have Come!

South Africa and Cuba in Today's World

NELSON MANDELA, FIDEL CASTRO

Speaking together in Cuba in 1991, Mandela and Castro discuss the unique relationship and example of the struggles of the South African and Cuban peoples. $8.95

Write for a free catalog. See front of pamphlet for addresses.

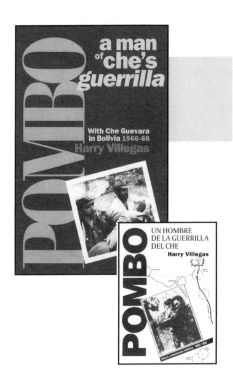

Pombo: a man of Che's *guerrilla*

With Che Guevara
in Bolivia, 1966–68

Harry Villegas's never-before published story of the revolutionary campaign in Bolivia led by Ernesto Che Guevara. It is the diary and account of Pombo — a member of Guevara's general staff, still in his twenties and already a veteran of a decade of struggle around the globe. The author is today a brigadier general in Cuba's Revolutionary Armed Forces. $21.95.

In Spanish published by
Editora Política. $18.95

The Bolivian Diary of Ernesto Che Guevara

Guevara's day-by-day chronicle of the guerrilla campaign in Bolivia, a painstaking effort to forge a continent-wide revolutionary movement of workers and peasants. Includes excerpts from the diaries and accounts of other combatants, including — for the first time in English — *My Campaign with Che* by Bolivian leader Inti Peredo, Introduction by Mary-Alice Waters. $21.95

Published In Spanish by
Editora Política as *El diario del Che en Bolivia*. $29.95